# FARTBOY
## THE FIRST SNIFF

**WARNING:**
NOT FOR THE
FAINT-FARTED

For my impro crew. You are the best—AW

To all the fart connoisseurs across the land, may your farts be forever stinky—JH

Scholastic Australia
An imprint of Scholastic Australia Pty Limited
PO Box 579 Gosford NSW 2250
ABN 11 000 614 577
www.scholastic.com.au

Part of the Scholastic Group
Sydney • Auckland • New York • Toronto • London • Mexico City • New Delhi • Hong Kong • Buenos Aires • Puerto Rico

Published by Scholastic Australia in 2020.

Cover design by Nicole Stofberg. Internal design by Keisha Galbraith.



A catalogue record for this book is available from the National Library of Australia

ISBN: 978-1-74383-261-5

Typeset in Bree.

Printed by McPherson's Printing Group, Maryborough, VIC.

Scholastic Australia's policy, in association with McPherson's Printing Group, is to use papers that are renewable and made efficiently with wood from responsibly managed sources, so as to minimise its environmental footprint.

MIX
Paper from responsible sources
FSC® C001695

The paper in this book is FSC® certified. FSC® promotes environmentally responsible, socially beneficial and economically viable management of the world's forests.

21 22 23 24 25 / 2

# FARTBOY

## THE FIRST SNIFF

ADAM WALLACE

JAMES HART

A Scholastic Australia Book

# The Boy Who Never Farts

My name is Martin. Martin Kennedy.

I live in Sparkletown, which has been the **world's tidiest town** for seventeen years straight! Everything in Sparkletown is neat and tidy and clean and sparkly and shiny.

The **houses** are neat and tidy and clean and sparkly and shiny.

**Mr Hamilton's head** is neat and tidy and clean and sparkly and shiny.

Even the rubbish is neat and tidy and clean and sparkly and shiny.

**Everything** is neat and tidy and clean and sparkly and shiny!

This is perfect for me, because I love being neat and tidy and clean and sparkly and shiny **SOOOOOOO MUCH!**

I am on the **Tidy Town Committee**, and I am also on the **Anti-Gross Committee.**

Gross things are stinky and smelly and slimy and yucky and I don't like them . . . **AT ALL!**

In fact, I don't like gross things ***so much*** that I have never, in my **whole entire life,** not once—I don't think I can even say the word, but I will—I have never, ever, ever **farted.** And I never, ever will.

I am the **cleanest,** most ungross kid in the world.

And that is why the only bad thing about Sparkletown is **THE FACTORY** on the outskirts of town.

It is, of course, a very neat and tidy and clean and sparkly and shiny **FACTORY.**

It sells **millions of dollars'** worth of product every single year.

It gives many people work, including my awesome mum and dad.

Basically, if it wasn't for **THE FACTORY,** Sparkletown probably would not exist!

So why is **THE FACTORY** bad?

Well, **THE FACTORY** that is so crucial to our town makes and sells the most **fart-creating food** in the whole entire world . . .

Sparkletown is actually responsible for **ninety-eight** per cent of the world's farts!

It's **so weird.** And it's also the reason I am telling you my story.

# IT'S TIDY TOWN TIME!

The second Monday of spring is a very important day in Sparkletown. It is three months before the judging panel from the **World's Tidiest Town Judging Committee** comes to judge us with their judging.

Three months to tidy like we have never tidied before.

Three months to make shiny things shine and sparkly things sparkle!

The **BEST** three months of my **LIFE.**

At 4 p.m., I was going to the Town Hall for our monthly **Tidy Town** meeting, when Mrs Jansen appeared.

Mrs Jansen was the only person who took tidiness more seriously than me. She was the **tidiest adult** in the whole, entire world. But suddenly she did not look good.

**'MARTIN, IT'S A DISASTER!'**

she said.

'What's wrong, Mrs Jansen?'

'It's the snacks for the meeting! They haven't arrived!'

Oh no. She was right. **This WAS a disaster!** We **always** have snacks! And they are always **awesome.**

'It's OK,' I said. 'I can go and get some for you. I have pocket money.'

Mrs Jansen pulled herself together. 'You're a good boy, Martin. But the thing is, there is **only one place** open today.'

NO. PLEASE DON'T SAY IT!
NO
NO
NO
NO
NO
NO
NO!
NO!
NO
NO
NO
NO
NO
NO
NO
NO!
No
NO

'THE BAKED BEANS FACTORY!'
NOOOOOOOO
OOOOOOOOOOOOOOOO
OOOOOOOOOOOOOO!!!

I had never been to **THE BAKED BEANS FACTORY.**

I didn't go to Mother-Son Days or Father-Son Days or Baked-Beans-Eating-Competition Days or After-Baked-Beans-Eating-Competition-Farting-Competition Days **or any days!**

But now, here I was, about to go to **THE BAKED BEANS FACTORY** on the outskirts of town **for the first time.** At least I would see Mum and Dad there. And at least I would get back in time for the **Tidy Town meeting.**

And at least it was a sunny day and the air smelt fresh.

Basically, everything was great and **nothing could go wrong.**

# THE POOP HITS THE HAZE

I arrived at **THE FACTORY** to find a strange haze covering the whole building.

Uh-oh. **What was going on?**

Smoke from the chimneys? No. Sparkletown is **pollution-free.**

A mirage because it was so hot? No, the weather was cool and pleasant. It was a **perfect day.**

And then, as I got closer, I realised what it was. No. Not realised. **Smelt.**

It was just after afternoon tea. Everyone at **THE FACTORY** had just eaten baked beans. The haze was from their stinky, rotten, gross, disgusting, post-baked-beans-eating fart gas and it smelt

**SO BAD!**

I lifted my shirt up over my mouth and nose. I sucked in a **deep breath.** I put my cleaning safety goggles on.

I leant forward, took one step and fell over. Seriously, **the stench** was that rotten! How did anyone work there?

I sat up and looked at the building. I had to get in there and get snacks. I couldn't let Mrs Jansen down.

I staggered to my feet. And then, through my goggles, I saw a **bird** flying over **THE FACTORY.**

I saw the bird do a **poop.**

I saw the poop drop from the sky straight towards **THE FACTORY'S** chimney.

At exactly the same time, Mr Hamilton was walking back to his security post.

The sun glinted off his shiny head, creating a **supercharged sunbeam** that shot straight towards the falling bird poop.

If the supercharged sunbeam ignited the bird poop, and then the flaming bird poop hit the fart gas cloud . . . **the result would be catastrophic!**

I started running. I had to get Mum and Dad out of **THE FACTORY.**

At that moment, the supercharged sunbeam hit the poop and it **burst into flames.**

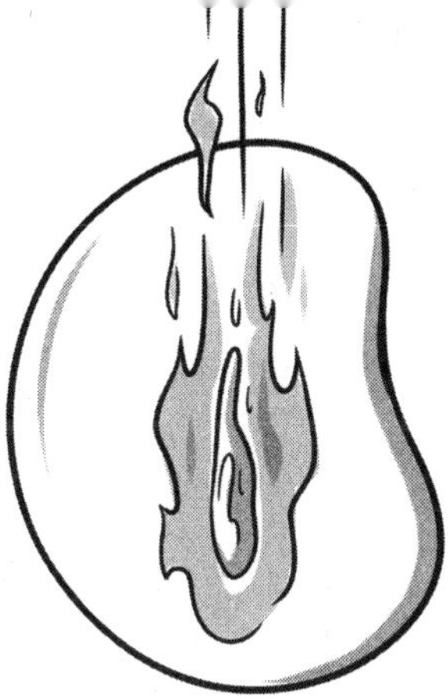

I reached inside Mr Hamilton's security booth and pressed the **evacuation** button.

The flaming poop got closer. Workers flooded out of the building.

I raced against the flow of people, towards **THE FACTORY.** As I got to the main door someone yelled out, 'Martin?'

**'MUM!'** As I ran towards her, I looked up. And that's when I saw the **flaming hot poop** hit the **fart-gas cloud.**

KA-P

OOOM!

There was a mighty, stinky **explosion** that sounded like a **mega whoopie cushion.**

The force threw me up into the air, and I flew for about fifty metres before . . . everything went black.

# Dr Doctor, Give me the news

I woke up in the hospital.

No-one knew I was awake, but I could hear bits of conversations going on around me.

'What's that smell?'

'HAVE YOU GOT ANY BAKED BEANS?'

'Baked beans everywhere!'

'Who let the dogs out?'

'I'm really hungry!'

'Parents missing . . .'

**Opening my eyes,** I saw doctors and nurses and assistants and a dog that had been let out. As soon as everyone realised I was awake, they began to speak at once.

MARTIN!

How are you feeling?

Are you OK?

My tummy felt **really weird**, and I was kind of **dizzy**, but that was it.

'Martin,' one of the doctors finally said, shushing the others. 'I am **Dr Doctor**.'

Your surname is Doctor?
Yes.
And you're a doctor?
Yes.
That is so cool!
Yes.

Dr Doctor the doctor changed the topic. 'Martin, I am so sorry to tell you this, but after the explosion, well, your parents . . .'

'What about my parents?' I asked.

Dr Doctor sighed, then spoke again. 'I'm afraid we can't find them. **Your parents are missing.**'

Wait, what? ***Missing?*** **My parents?**

Dr Doctor put a hand on my shoulder. 'They will be found, Martin, and they will be OK. I am sure of that. Until then, you will live with your grandmother.'

**Grandmother?** I didn't even know I *had* a grandmother! I tried to speak, but I couldn't find the words. **'But,'** I said. **'But-but-but-but . . .'**

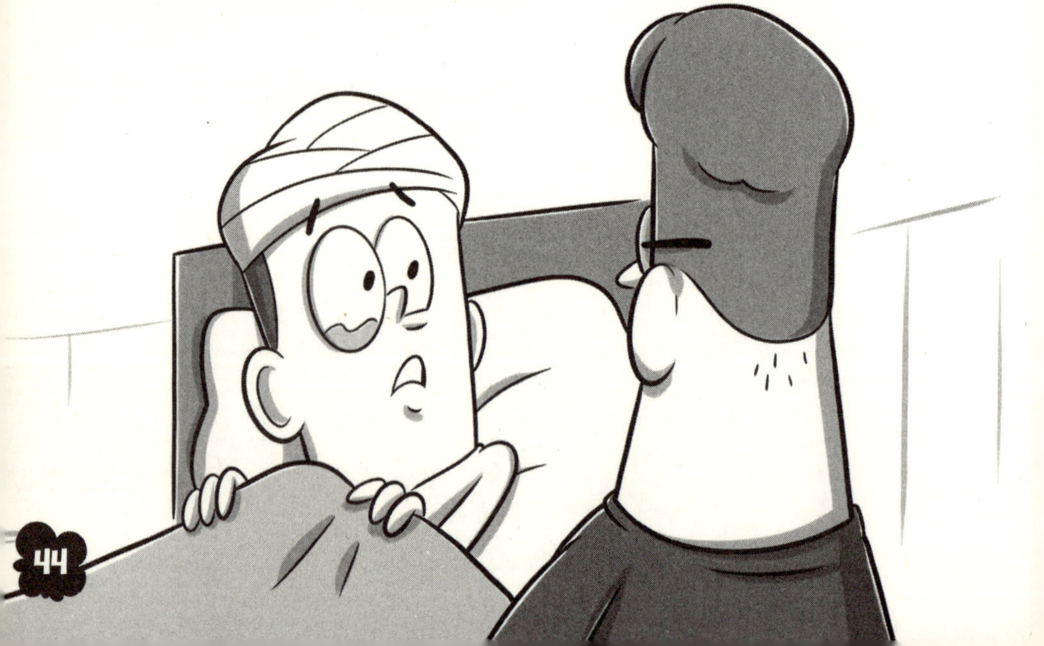

‘Yes,’ Dr Doctor said. ‘We need to talk **about your butt.** There is more bad news. You were in a big explosion, Martin. You are lucky to be alive. But you may notice some . . . changes.’

‘Changes like what?’ I asked.

My tummy was **definitely feeling weird.** It was gurgling, too.

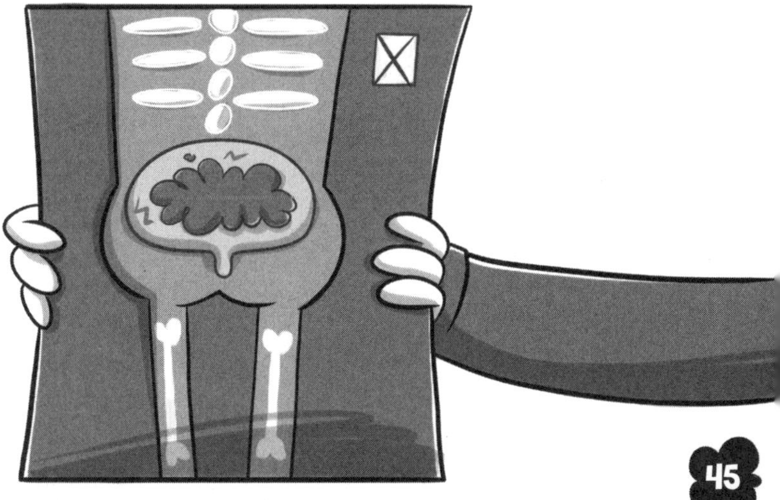

'Well, for starters,' Dr Doctor said. 'You may find that you now begin to—'

'No,' I said. 'Don't say it. Don't say it, Doc.'

**'You may begin to—'**

**'Your butt may—'**

**'I DON'T WANNA HEAR IT!'**

**'FART!'** he cried. **'YOU WILL FART LIKE EVERYONE ELSE IN THE WORLD!'**

**'NOOOOOOOOOOOOOOOOOO!'**

This was the worst news ever. *Me? Farting?* **No, no, no, no, no, no, NO!**

As I tried to take everything in, the door flew open, and **an old lady** walked into the room. When she saw me, her eyes narrowed.

**'MARTIN?'**

I nodded.

**'The boy who never farts?'**

'That's right,' I said. **'Never.'**

'Oh, he will,' Dr Doctor said. 'Soon he will be popping like a balloon.'

The old lady's face broke into a huge grin. 'Oh boy,' she said. 'Martin, I'm your **long-lost grandma.** We're going to have some fun.'

# Grandma Lets Rip

Grandma was my dad's mother. I had never met her before, except for when I was a baby. After that, she had been travelling the world. But now, since I would be going to live with her, she had moved to **Sparkletown.**

I was still really sad that my parents were missing, so at first I didn't want to leave my home. But then I learned that Grandma was **super neat.**

Her house was **SO TIDY!**

She showed me my room, which was **really nice.**

She showed me her yard, which was **perfectly mown.**

She showed me her cupboards, where everything was arranged in **perfect order.**

## She was just like me!

'So,' Grandma said. 'You have never passed wind before?'

I hung my head in shame. 'Never. But now I might. I'm sorry, Grandma.'

Grandma lifted my chin and made me look at her. 'Seriously? Never once?'

I shook my head.

For such a neat lady, Grandma was kind of gross.

Where was she coming up with these?

'Never caused a **VOLCANIC ERUPTION** on Uranus? Never dropped a **WHOPPER?** Never been Alexander Popoff? Never been a **LEAN, MEAN, FARTING MACHINE?** Never cut the cheese, exploded a **BUTT BOMB**, had a **BACK-END BLOWOUT**, were **LOUD AND DEADLY**, roared from the rear, **FAAAAAARRRRRRRRRRTED?'**

I sighed. 'No, Grandma.'

'Martin, look around you. This place is kind of tidy, right?'

'It's wonderful, Grandma,' I said, glad to be talking about tidiness now.

'Well, it's all a front, m'boy.'

And then my neat and tidy long-lost grandma **lifted her leg and let rip** with a whopper of a fart! I couldn't believe it!

'At least it doesn't smell,' I said.

Grandma laughed. 'Oh, Martin! It seems that explosion destroyed your sense of smell. The pong in here is like seventy-nine dead rats rotting in a muddy puddle of **rotten dog poop.**'

'Oh.'

'And then they died three years ago.'

'Oh.'

'And so they are **stinky.**'

'Yeah. I got that.'

‘And then the **dead zombie rats** ate **garlic** and **rotten eggs** and **breathed right in our faces.**’

‘Wow.’

‘It’s not going away, either. That’s a **lingerer.**’

Was she really **so gross?** Maybe we weren't alike after all. I didn't know if this was going to work. And really, I just wanted to be with my parents again. And I would **never, EVER pop off.**

Grandma sensed I was upset. 'Martin, let's go sit outside.'

We did.

'Wow, that smell's following us. That was **one of my best!'** Grandma grabbed her walking stick. 'Let's take a walk to the lake.'

Even after everything that had happened, little did I know that **my entire world** was about to change . . . again (even more!).

# Never say never

'I may be an old fart,' Grandma said as we walked, 'but every now and then my **trouser tuba** tunes up. Here's the thing, though. No-one ever knows it is me. I have learnt to **control my pops.** I only drop a whopper if there is a dog or someone I don't like near me, so I can blame them.'

I was shocked. 'Really?'

'Really. And I can do all sorts of different pops, too. **LOUD**, silent, **FRIENDLY**, **DEADLY**—I have a full range, and now you, sweet, gentle Martin, soon you will be tooting with the best of them.'

'But I don't want to! It's so gross!'

Grandma stopped walking. She turned to face me. 'Martin. To pass wind is a natural thing. But we need to learn to control it. I will train you. I will be your **methane mentor.** Your **butt-sneeze supervisor.** Your **gassy guru.**'

**'NO!'** I said. 'Never! You don't get it, Grandma! **I . . . WILL . . .**

# NEVER . . . FART!'

As I said the last word, Grandma popped a spoonful of something into my mouth.

Then, before I even realised what was happening, I swallowed it.

My tummy **gurgled** and **rumbled** and **squelched.** I looked around. We were at the lake. There were people everywhere, walking, playing, swimming, kayaking.

I gritted my teeth to try and stop it, I really did. **But it was no use.**

A teeny . . . tiny . . . bit of warm gas escaped my rear end.

'NOOOOOOOOOOOOOOOOOOOOOOOOOO!'

It had only been **a little fart**, but I was so embarrassed.

I went to ask Grandma what she'd fed me, but she was out cold!

# IT WAS DESTINY, NO BUTTS ABOUT IT

**'GRANDMA!'** I cried. **'ARE YOU OKAY?'**

I poured my bottle of water over her face, and she woke up, spluttering. I thought she would be angry, but her face broke into a huge grin . . .

'It was tiny,' I said. 'And embarrassing.'

'Tiny? Look around, Martin.'

I looked. There was a circle of **wilted flowers** around me, and eighty-seven **dead ants.**

I dropped to my knees. **'WHAT HAVE I DONE?'**

'Martin, I—' Grandma didn't get a chance to finish her sentence. She was cut off by a scream.

# 'AAARRRGGGHHH!'

We both spun around. A woman's kayak had **tipped over** and she was struggling, way out in the lake.

Grandma gazed at the woman, horrified. 'Martin, you have to help her!'

'How can I help? It will take me ages to swim out there.'

'This is your **destiny!**' Grandma exclaimed.

*My destiny?* I was so confused.

Grandma's eyes lit up as she held out a container. 'This is what I put in your mouth. Just one of them. **EAT A FEW.**'

I opened the container. ***No.***

No, no, no, no, no, no, **NO!**

Inside the container were . . . **baked beans!** This was **my worst nightmare!**

Some lifeguards were paddling towards the woman, but they were too far away. They would arrive too late.

'You have to do this,' Grandma said, walking me to the edge of the water. 'It is your destiny. This is your time!'

**What was Grandma talking about?**

People with jet skis and boats were driving out to help the struggling woman, but no-one was near her yet.

And now she was getting tired and starting to sink.

Was this *really* my destiny? I reached in, took one bean and closed my eyes. Very slowly, **I put the bean into my mouth.**

# Fartin' Martin to the Rescue

I bit the bean. It actually tasted quite nice, but as soon as I swallowed, my tummy reacted. It *gurgled*. It **GROANED**.

Grandma put on a *gas mask* and moved upwind.

That's when I did the biggest, loudest, most powerful **bottom burp** ever!

It was like **all the farts** I had never done **happened at once.**

A puppy was **blown** into the air.

A **skunk** fell in love.

I went **ZOOMING** across the water towards the lady.

I **BLEW** past the swimmers.

I **BLASTED** through the ducks.

In fact, I farted myself straight past the woman I was trying to save! I couldn't stop. **I was out of control.**

I put a hand in the water to slow myself down, but it didn't work. Instead I went round and round in **stinky circles**, creating a whirlpool.

And all the people in the whirlpool started feeling sick.

I clenched my cheeks.

Nothing happened.

**NO! YOUR BUTT CHEEKS!**

Oh. That made much more sense, but it was too late.

**A lady spewed** which made **another person spew** which made **everyone on a boat spew** which made **a whale spew!**

I squeezed my **butt cheeks** together until the **roar of my fart** lessened to a squeak that sounded like a mouse snoring.

I looked around and saw what my fart had accomplished . . . **the woman was safe!**

**'MARTIN!'** Grandma screamed. **'LOOK OUT!'**

I turned around. My wind had produced an unexpected side-effect. A **GIANT WAVE** was coming towards me.

**'IT'S A POONAMI!'** Grandma screamed. **'It's like a tsunami, but it stinks, so I used the word poo instead!'**

'We got it, Grandma,' I yelled, kicking my legs furiously to get away.

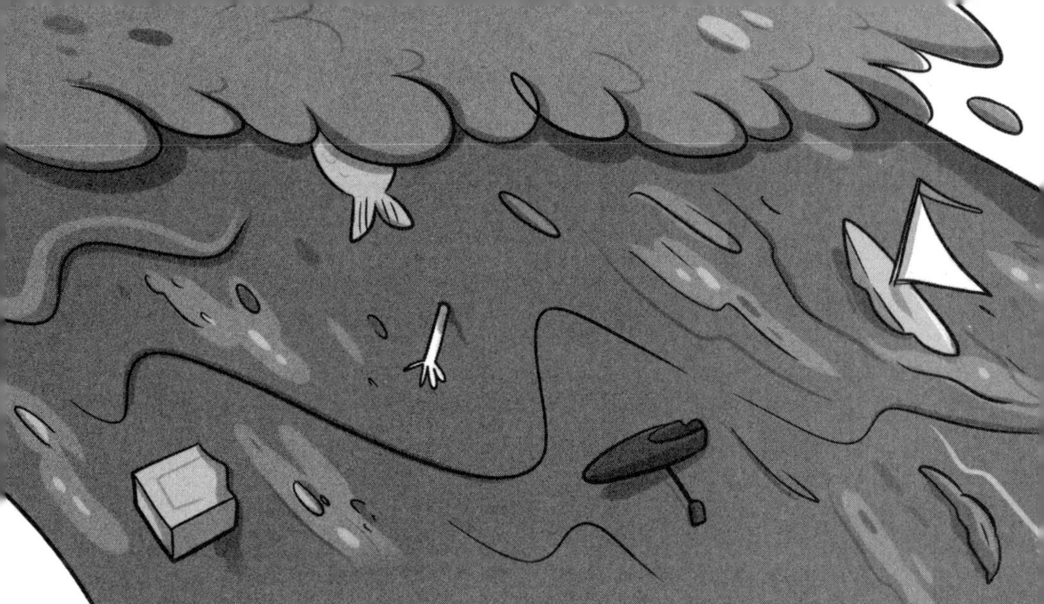

**'FART, MARTIN! FART AND SEND IT BACK TO WHERE IT CAME FROM!'**

I tried. I really did. I pushed and I squeezed, but nothing happened. I was out of gas. The wave would wash us all away. My fart had saved one woman, but it was about to **destroy the town!**

# The Poonami

I didn't know what to do. The giant wave was coming towards us. People were swimming away, partly to escape from the wave, partly to get out of all the **chunky vomit** in the water.

Then I heard a roar.

I checked my butt. Nope, wasn't me. Which was good. **Because I was done.** I had never used to fart, and now every fart was a disaster.

My parents were still gone, and soon my new home with Grandma would be too. I was in spewy water. People were about to drown and it was all my fault.

The wave got **BIGGER.**

And **CLOSER.** So did the roar.

Was this the end?

Then I saw a jet ski racing towards me, its motor roaring. And on the jet ski was . . . Grandma?

**Seriously?**

But it was. She raced up to me and stopped. **'GET ON,'** she said.

I got on.

Then she started up again, but she didn't zoom towards land . . .

**. . . she zoomed towards the poonami!**

'Grandma!' I screamed. 'What are you doing?'

'It's time, Martin,' she said. 'It's time to **unleash the beast.**'

'Do you mean that shark in front of us with its mouth open ready to eat us?'

'No, but—**AAAGGGHHH!'** She turned and dodged the shark, who snapped its jaws shut and got a mouthful of watery vomit.

**'I can't do it, Grandma, I can't do it again. *I hate it.*'**

The jet ski sputtered to a halt as the poonami drew in all the water from the lake. The water was now only knee deep.

'You have been given a gift,' Grandma explained. 'A **gross, stinky gift,** but a gift all the same. But with great stinkiness comes great responsibility.'

She spread out an arm. 'Look at all those people swimming through spew-filled water, trying to get away. **YOU CAN HELP THEM!'**

I looked. It was disgusting.

**'I CAN'T, GRANDMA. I JUST CAN'T.'**

Grandma tried a different tack. 'The people will all be washed away. We have to save them.'

She held out a spoonful of **baked beans.** 'If we don't stop this poonami . . . Sparkletown will be filthy!'

I groaned. She was right. If the poonami hit, this wouldn't be the world's tidiest town anymore. **I almost cracked.**

Then Grandma played her trump card.

'Martin, if we don't stop that wave, we may **never find your parents.**'

My parents. My wonderful, loving, missing parents.

# Beans, Beans, Good for your Heart

I opened my mouth and Grandma shoved the spoon in. I chewed and swallowed. I knew what one bean had done. What would a **whole spoonful** do? I was about to find out.

A **rumble** started in my tummy.

The rumble became a **roar**.

Grandma aimed **my butt** at the poonami, which was really close now.

People were screaming
and swimming
and paddling.

My entire body shook. My eyes watered. The **poonami** rushed closer!

I couldn't do it though. I was freaking out.

**'YOU HAVE TO LET IT GO!'** Grandma screamed, holding me as steady as she could. **'YOU HAVE TO UNCLENCH!'**

Huh?

**Hero?**

Because of my stinky butt?

I looked at my **beautiful town**, about to be destroyed. I stared at all the people trying to get to safety. I thought of **my parents**, and I knew that if everything was washed away, I would never find them. I couldn't let that happen.

I relaxed my muscles and just **let it go.**

Grandma held me like I was a cannon, and my fart **blasted** against the poonami.

**'BRAAAAPPPT!!!'** I roared from my mouth and my butt.

It was a standstill,
**FART VERSUS WAVE.**
Neither one more
powerful than the other.

But Grandma wasn't taking any chances. She poured **the whole can** of baked beans into my open mouth.

A fart the size of a nuclear bomb **exploded from my bum.** Me and Grandma went flying, and the poonami shot straight up into the air . . . before crashing down with **a mighty splash.**

POOOM!!

# FARTBOY

We washed up on the sand at the edge of the lake. And when I finally got up, I saw that the water was calm.

Everyone cheered . . . until the stink from the **mighty butt bomb** hit them!

Then people groaned and ran for cover, **blocking their noses** and **crying for their mummies.** One guy even sniffed a love-drunk skunk for relief.

But Grandma ignored all of that. She put a hat on my head, grabbed my arm and pretended to look frail. She shuffled away with me, heading back towards her house.

As soon as we were clear of the people, she dropped the disguise.

'Martin, that was amazing. **You're a hero.** But for your own protection, people can't know that it was you who saved them.'

But Grandma ignored my confusion. 'There are **three things** you need,' she continued. 'First, **a costume**, to hide your real identity.'

We tried
a lot of
costumes.

Some were a **maybe.**

Some were a **NO!**

But Grandma finally gave the thumbs-up. 'Next, you need a catch-cry.'

'Really?'

'Yes, for when you **fluff into action.** How about . . .'

'Ew. No.' I didn't like that at all.

'OK, maybe . . .'

'Grandma, that's disgusting.'

'Martin, remember, this isn't *you*, it's you as a *superhero*,' she said.

She was right, but I didn't even know if I *wanted* to be a superhero. Not like this anyway. But I decided to say yes to her next offer.

Hmmm. Maybe the one *after* that.

And so I had a catch-cry.

'What's the **third thing**, Grandma?' I was actually starting to enjoy this a bit.

Grandma smiled. 'You need a **hero name.**'

'Oooooh, I got this one!' I said, ready to throw some gross words at her. **'Stinky botty?'**

'No.'

**'Gasboy?'**

'No.'

The lid was open and the words poured out.

I was on a roll!

'FARTBOY! YOUR HERO NAME IS FARTBOY!'

'Yes, Grandma. Sorry, Grandma.'

'It's OK, Martin. It's been a big day.'

# LET'S ROCK THIS FARTY!

I laid my new costume on the bed. Could I *really* be a hero?

I sighed. I wished Mum and Dad were here.

Grandma was watching the news.

'A super villain, calling herself **Madam Wax,** has robbed the Sparkletown National Bank. She turned the guards into statues using massive amounts of her own earwax. She **will** strike again. **Who** will stop her?'

'In other **other** news, there are still people missing after **THE BAKED BEANS FACTORY** explosion.'

And that was when I knew. If there were dirtbags in the area, if my beloved town needed a hero to clean it up, who better than **the world's tidiest kid?** I still thought my **fart power** was **gross,** but maybe I could use it for good and not evil.

I went and put my costume on and stood in front of the mirror.

*Yeah.*

*I can do this.*

*I can be Fartboy.*

THE FARTS WILL GO ON!
Stay tuned for the next adventure of . . .
FARTBOY
F